$100 in 24 hours on the Internet:

You can earn $100 in 24 hours on the Internet. There is no magic button. It takes work but you can do it. Earn means you have completed the work and the money is owed to you. With some of the companies included in this report as resources, payment is on a weekly or monthly basis.

Many times, working with individuals, the payment will be made immediately upon completion of the work. The 24 hours begins the minute you decide to start work. You don't need any up front cash to get started, just your wits, a computer and an Internet connection. It's a given you have the needed software for word processing, but if you don't you can download Open Office.

Just to be clear, this report is not advising you to gather up all your un used books, videos, games, whatever, and sell them on Ebay. That is a way to generate cash, but no different than a garage sale, it's just online. This report is about earning the money from scratch. There are a few basics you will need to have in place. You probably already have a Paypal account, but if you don't set one up. You can accept payment through Paypal for the most part, unless it's a commission for an affiliate sale. If that's the case, set up accounts at Commission Junction and Clickbank. Set up an account at craigslist and us free ads. You will be using it for placing ads.

There is no cost for the account, or for the ads. All of this should take no more than an hour, so

you've got 23 hours left. If you are planning to sell a

product, whether it's your own, or someone else's product and receive a commission, set up a blog, squidoo page, or hubpage.

More about blogging and squidooing later. Part Two of this report includes ways you can

continue to earn $100 a day over the long term. There is no guarantee that you will earn any
money at all, that depends on you. Earn $100 in 24 hours today Make Money Ghost Writing
articles You have to have some writing

talent to ghost write articles. You do need to be _____ ed, able to research topics quickly, summarize the main points and write the article in a clear way, with correct spelling and grammar. The article length can

range from 200 words to
1000 words or more. Payment is usually by the word. For beginners, a 500 word article can be
sold for about $5.00. An accomplished ghost writer can charge up to $50 for a 500 word article.

The client gives you the topic and any key words that must be included in the article. How long it takes to write t he article is dependent upon how mu ch you alread y know about t he topic and how quickly you can find the materials you

need to research the topic. It is possible, working at
a steady pace, to write twenty 400-500 word articles in one day. That's $100 at $5 per article.
Both Digital Point and The Warrior Forum, have   threads where

people offer their services for sale. You can post an offer at no cost on Digital Point but you have to have been a member and have 15 posts to your name in order to do so. WarriorForum also requires that you have been a member for awhile and there is a fee to post a WSO. However, you can still earn money through these boards. Join both of these groups. Scan the posts on the WSO thread and the

Buy-Sell-Trade board at Digital Point. Offer your services to the people who are asking questions
about the services currently offered, or who have said they've bought the service. Do this by
the private message function on both

boards, not by posting on the thread. Place ads on craigslist and usfreeads offering your service. Other forums where you may find clients SitePoint.com www.v7n.com www.webtalkforums.com/

www.talkfreelance.com/

www.associateprograms.com

www.wickedfire.com/im4newbies.com/forum/

www.wahm.com/forum/

www.internetbasedmoms.com/bb/www.businessforum.net/

Post on forums It has been shown that people don't want to post on forums unless there are already posts. New forum owners pay people to post comments, start

threads, and respond to
other threads in an effort to get some forum action going. As the forum grows, the level of posting increases until paid posts aren't necessary. Forum topics have a huge variety. There's

probably a forum for just about any subject. Usually a paid poster has to have at least some knowledge of the subject to post relevant comments. There can be a minimum word count for the posts. Posts of "I agree," "Me too," and "Thanks for the info," are too short and don't add anything to the discussion, so forum owners don't want to pay for them. Posting on forums doesn't pay a lot, perhaps as little as 10 posts for a dollar. Find the jobs on Internet marketing related web sites like Digital Forum. Post on blogs You can be paid to post comments on blogs much the same way you can be paid to post on forums. Pretty

much the same criteria applies,
the posts can't be too short and have to be relevant to the subject matter. You can search for
offers of 5 posts for a dollar. If each post takes a minute you would have to work a little over 8

hours to make $100. Place ads on craigslist and use free ads offering your service.

Writing Articles for Pay There are sites that pay for content. Most of the sites require that you post your article first and wait for a buyer to come by to purchase your articles. Associated Content buys the article from you. The pay is minimal from $3 to $5 per 500 word article. However there are occasions where Associated Content has paid up to $50

per article. The articles can be
submitted on an exclusive basis, meaning they aren't and won't be posted anywhere else, or

ich
d the

article elsewhere. It takes a day or two for Associated Content to review the article and make the offer. You are not req uired to accept the
offer and can withdraw the article. It takes another two days for the article to be published and

then two or three days for Associated Content to make the payment to you . Place ads on craigslist and use free ads offering your service. Websites that pay for articles: associated

content constant-content helium life tips how to do things
http://www.shvoong.com
http://www.articlewarehouse.com http://www.authorconnection.com

There are a number of sites you can post articles, tips, or essays to. You get paid a share of the earnings of the ads that show up with your article. The more popular your art icle, the more views, the more revenue you can earn. Sites that share ad revenue with writers www.flixya.com /

www.daytipper.com
www.metacafe.com/

www.vume.com/
www.hubpages.com

Pay Per Sale, Affiliate Programs, and Commissions You're simply selling someone else's product through your marketing efforts, whether it's you r blog or web site, and you receive a sales commission when the sale is completed. Most of these products are infor mational, eit her an ecourse, software, or ebook. Quite a few o f the affiliate products pay more than a 50% commission. The smart product owners offer banners, buttons, sales copy, and even articles that you can use to promote with. Clickbank is one of the most estab lished programs. Commission Junction is another source. Both of these make the payment s to the affiliates so you don't have to worry whether the product owner will pay. PayDotCom is a program which uses PayPal as the payment method. The product owner makes the decision to pay the affiliates and has to authorize PayDotCom to do so. Many products offer their own affiliate program

independently look for one with a solid history of payment . You can also become an affiliate of amazon.com to sell books and consumer products such as jewelry, televisions, or other
consumer products. commission is much

lower, but sometimes the retail price is high enough to

make up for it. The fastest way to make money selling affiliate products is to think about the

forums, list s and discussion groups you already belong to, what are the qu estions being asked?

Is there a problem that people need a solution for? What are the hot topics? Set up an affiliate account at clickbank. Go to their market place and search for p roducts that will solve the problems, or are the answer to the questions being discussed. Set up a blog or squidoo pages that relate to the affiliate programs. Post a informative response and include a link to your blog

or website where you offer the affiliate product you are currently using. A softer sell is to post a review of the product on you r blog and then post a response to the list/discussion forum stating
that you've reviewed the product and they

can find out more on your blog. You can also set up a squidoo page and refer people to your squidoo page. You will probably need to make 3 to 4 sales to earn $100 in com missions.
Develop Your Own

Product This is the way you can make real money on the Internet. The question is: Can you do it in 24 hours? It would be very difficu lt to research a niche or market, decide what need is hottest and that you have the knowledge for, write the report, write the ad copy or sales letter, set up a blog/website/squidoo page and then market the report. In the real world in real time, it's not feasible. What you can do while you're working on the other ways to make $100 in

24 hours is jot down ideas you have that would the

basis for a product. Then when you have the time you can start developing the product. You

can develop a short report, 2500 words or so, a long report, 2500

to 5000 words, or an ebook,
7500 words and up. You could also develop an ecourse that's a combination of emails, an ebook, chats, and perhaps conference calls. Resources: Dave Lovelace's Quick & Easy Info

product Creation Guide How To Write Your Own Ebook. Get Paid to take sur veys online, Receive Offers, Read Email First rule don't pay someone to find out information about the "Get Paid To"

companies. There are too many sites which falsely represent that you will be paid cash for
taking surveys, referring visitors, or accepting offers. Some of these offers require a credit card.

You sign up for a free month of XYZ movies, get paid $15 for accepting the offer and provide your cred it card number. If you don't cancel the offer your credit will be billed, and you can't cancel immediately, or you won't be paid.

Usually you have to reach a minimum level of earnings to receive a check or deposit to your Paypal account. And the minimum level is nearly impossible to earn. Some of the surveys can be completed quickly and some take an hour or so to complete. Most of the money is made through referring other people. It will be a huge challenge to earn $100 in 24 hours, so there aren't any resources listed in this report . Blog Your

Way to Beaucoup Bucks. Blogging is a web site (don't worry you don't really need complex website skills) that you update everyday with posts about your chosen subject on your mind or schedule. Visitors can comment on

your posts for others to see. Using your blog as a billboard there are several websites who will pay you to post product reviews on your blog. They are paid
by the company who owns the products. The products can

range from consumer durable goods, consumable goods, or just about anything you can think of. The blog has to be approved by the company and has to remain up for a specified length of time. There usually has to be a qualifying statement that your post is a paid advertisement. Using your blog as a review site

Another way to use your blog is to p ost product reviews of affiliate products. When someone buys the product you're paid a commission. You can post reviews of books you've read that are available on amazon.com and link to the books as an affiliate. Ads on your blog If your blog has some what of a following in a certain niche and gets a reasonable amount of traffic, you can use pay per click (PPC) ads to generate some revenue. The more traffic to your blog, the higher the potential for click throughs, the more money you can earn. AdSense by Google is a very popular

PPC company but there are others. You can also use a blog to sell products as an affiliate. Live JournalBloggerhttp://www.wordpress.com are just a few of the free sites where you can quickly and easily set up your blog. Pick a market niche you're familiar with as the top ic for your blog.

Every d ay post on you r blog. Of course that's not all you need to do. You have to get people to
your blog to read it and hopefully click on your paid ads, or on

the products you're promoting as an affiliate. Most of the blog sites are searchable by key words. Search on the same words you've used for your site to find other blogs. Then leave a comment on the relevant blogs and

include your link to your own blog. You can submit your blog's url to search engines so if
someone wants infor mationon 'how to raise guppies' and that's the subject of your blog, your blog shows upfor visitors to find. With

a little bit of research and time you can become successful and increase you r bank account with Online Marketing just by blogging. Get paid to blog : blogerwave.com/bloggingads.com/www.blogsvertise.com/www.blo

gburst.com/www.blogtopro fit.com/www.buyablogger.com/ www.linkworth.com/loudlaunch.com/payperpost.com/payu2blog.com/www.reviewme.com/smorty.com/sponsoredreview.com/

Resources: Blogging to the Bank 2.0. Submitting Links to Articles, Websites and Blogs to Social Networking Sites. You can submit links to other people's articles, etc. to the social networking sites. The pay isn't terrific, usually no more than a couple of dollars per article. You'll have to set up an account at each

site. Below is a list to get you started. With a bit of research you can find quite a few more.

Offer the service on Digital Point the same

as you would offer to ghost write articles. Setting up the accounts at the social networking sites will probably take a couple of hours. If each article takes 20 minutes to post at all the social networking sites and you charge $4 for the service. You'd earn $12 an hour and would have to work a little over 9 hours to earn $100. You need your client to tell you the url of the article/website, title, brief description or first paragraph of the article, category, and tags or key words. Social Bookmarking sites

blinklist.com
stumbleupon.com
gnolia.com
linkagogo.com
wink.com
digg.com
technorati.com
newsvine.com

furl.net
backflip.com
spurl.net
netvouz.com
diigo.com
rawsugar.com
shadows.com

_____
_____ ıs
_____ s
_____ Ads for other
_____ ıe of the free
_____ rive traffic
_____

to your own site, or blog, is to post classified ads on ad sites. Craigslist is one of the most popular, and it seems effective, of the free ad sites. It is city specific, meaning you can only post your ad to one city at atime. But if

you're clever and reword the headline of the ad, and the body of thead, you can post to a
number of different cities as long as you use a different ad for each city. You can also po st ads
for people and get paid for it. The pay is

minimal, but the work doesn't take long after you 've set up accounts at the different ad sites.

    Other Classified Ad Sites Include :

http://www.highlandclassifieds.com/

http://www.usfreeads.com /

http://www.adlandpro.com/

http://www.pressmania.com /

http://www.wikalo.com/

http://www.mocca.com/

http://www.adlot.net/

http://www.effectlocal.com/

http://www.interking.com /

http://www.homeworkads.com/

http://www.classifiedsforfree.com/

http://www.1america
mall.com/
http://www.t
headnet.com/

_____
_____
_____
_____
_____

_____
com

ıssified2

ls.yaho

/base/
ls.mysp

e.com/
ckpage.

http://www.oodle.com/
http://www.adpost.com/
http://www.FreeAdvertisingForum.com
http://www.sell.com/
http://www.InetGiant

$100 a day, over the long term:

The above suggestions really

can earn you $100 in a 24 hour period if you work for it. The ways below take a little bit of time to get set up and get going but can earn you $100 a day in the long term. When approp riate put ads on craigslist and use free ads about your product orservice you're offering. Squidoo Lenses Think of squidoo as a place where you can get a free one page - but it can be avery long one page — website.

When setting up a squidoo lens, you first need todo some research on key words. Trust me this is important. So th ink about your squidoo lens and come up with 4 or 5 key word phrases. Pop them in Google and see what competition you 're up against. You can also go to Google's adword key word generator, https://adwords.google.com/select/KeywordToolExternal Use the tab key word variations, enter your key words and th en hit the "get more key words" tab to proceed next, pick out eight to ten key word phrases, these will be your tags. Now go to http://www.squidoo.com and get yourself a lens using your key word phrase as the name of the lens. Set up your bio in your bio module and link to your product or website in that module. Now write a 250 to 500 word essay using your key word phrase at least three times. The essay should be relevant to your product or niche. In the essay link to your product, affiliate product and/or to your website. You might want to use a teaser phrase to encourage people to click on the link. Add a poll and an amazon module, then add another text module with links to your other products or affiliate products. Add a Google news feed module. Then another text module and finally end with a guest book.

This may sound complicated but all the modules are clearly explained and it's really a matter of point and click to populate your lens with interesting products. You can earn money from your lens through the different modules and their products, such as books from amazon.com, from products that you're an affiliate for and from your own products. You can put up a lens for each one of your key word phrases and then link them together. Resources: Social Networking on Squidoo This eBook is by Tiffany Dow, one of the most well known and most successful Squidoo'ers to date. AdSense Google through their AdSense program, offers paid advertising through the use of text linked ads placed on websites. These ads can also be placed on blogs.

Advertisers h ope to convince visitors to click on the text ad and visit their own websites through these text linked ads. The advertisers pay Google for everyvisitor that clicks through. Google passes on some of the money to the owner of the web sites where the click originated. This is know as **PPC** or pay per click. Savvy Internet marketers build websites on topics that have a high PPC with the sole purpose of earning money. Some of these sites known as MFA or Made For AdSense contain little or nore deeming content. The website's own er's intent is to place high in

the search engines for a niche key word phras e. Say

"Natural Cures for Whatever." People have a tendency to only look at the first page of results when searching. They click on the "Natural Cures for Whatever" site. When they arrive there is little information, so in an effort to leave the site quickly, they click on one of the text lin ked ads to navigate away. A better philosophy is to make the site content rich to attract visitors and establisha level of trust. The visitor feels comfortable and when they've found the information they needed they are more likely to click on one of the text based ads. How much money can you earn with AdSense? It depends on the topic of your website, you r key word usage and your traffic. People look for all sorts of information on the Internet. Quite a bit of the time they're looking for a solution to a problem or how-to-do something. If your website addresses those issues, the odds are it will make more money than a generic site. You have to have a website already up and running before you apply for AdSense. They are accepting blogs for AdSense revenue as well. Once you get one blog orwebsite approved you can add the AdSense to your other sites/blogs without additional approval. Once you're app roved you have your choice of style and size of ad. You don't have to do any of the coding. You do have to know how to incorporate the cod e onyour website or blog.

It's not difficult, you can track how much money you 're making nearly in real time.

Resources:

10 Adsense Secrets to Triple Your CTRUse Forums and Discussion

Groups

You can join forums and discussion groups that relate to your website/blog/squidoo page. Search discussion group sites like http://yahoogroups.com and http://groups.google.c

om for groups that are relevant.

You can also search for discussion groups by subject matter. Type in the search engines +discussion +groups +mothers +young +children, for example. Another alternative is to find websites that relate to your website that have forums. There's a huge forum for writers at

AbsoluteWrite.com, for example. Many online publications on your topic will have forums as well. Join these discussion groups. In you r profile make sure you keep your signature short and sweet but do include a one sentence descrip tion of yoursite/blog /squidoo lens and a link. When questions come up, or the conversation focuses on your topic, you can post a short answer and then mention there is an article or suggestion that would be helpful to the members at your site and give the link. Of course don't spam the members or just post one or two word answers, like "thank you" or "I agree " just to post. Social Net working Sites Keep in mind the word networ king is a verb, and that means action. Go to facebook and set up a profile that reflects the product/website/affiliate product you want to sell. Keep the profile fun and interesting. You can also use the blogs online to update your current activities. You can add photos, videos from YouTube. games. Then search for friends using your key words to find people interested in your product. Say you have a golf product, search for golfers. If you have a recipe book, search for people who like to cook. You can also join the forums at

Myspace and look for friends that way. The advantage of having friends is that you can send bulletins to you r friends that will automatically be posted at their facebook profile and seen by all their friends. If you have 100 friends and they each have 100 friends, one of you r bullet ins can potentially be seen by 10,000 people. Ryze is social networking site that leans a little more toward business. Again setup your profile with you r links, t hen look for groups to join. The groups should be relevant to your website or products. Most groups have active discussions going on. Answer questions, ask questions and contribute to the discussion. There are lots of other social networking sites you can join. Every day spend a few minutes visiting each of your site's network.

Niche Marketing

Niche marketing is a buzz word and it simply means

marketing to a small niche rather than a _____

example: Your blog is about cures for sinus headaches, that's very broad. A narrower niche would be natural cures for sinus headaches and an even narrower niche is natural herbal cures for sinus headaches. The logic is that there are fewer blogs/websites competing for the very narrow niche than the much broader topic. There will be fewer people searching for natural herbal cures for sinus headaches but more of them will be ready to buy a product or click on an AdSense ad.

Resources: Micro Niche Finder, Bum Marketing, so bum marketing is simply using articles you've written to drive traffic to ablog/

website/squidoo page you've set up that sells an affiliate product, or your own product. The article is submitted to article directories and includes a bio box that has a little bit about you and the link to your

blog /website/squidoo page. The tricks to BUM Markeing are very simple. 1. Use key words in
the title of your article and in the article itself so people searching for those key word s will find
your article on the major search engines.

2. Make the article informative and interesting, but leave t he readers wanting more. 3. Include a teaser in your bio box that entices the reader to click on the link to your website/blog. 4. Write enough articles

using those keywords. How much is enough? A rule of thumb is one article per day for the first month.

Article Directories - EzineArticles (By far, the be st)
http://www.articledashboard.com

http://www.isnare.com
http://www.goarticles.com
http://www.buzzle.com
http://www.articlesfactory.com
http://www.articlefinders.com
http://www.articlecity.com
http:// www.article-

planet.comhttp://www.market ing-seek.comhttp://www.ezadsuccess.comResources:Bum Marketing Method Travis Sago is the undisputed king of Bum Marketing, and his incredibly detailedand informative eCourse is absolutely free .Now you have lots of ways to earn $100 in

24 hours and over the long term. I hope you 're successful with your Internet Marketing efforts. Just keep in mind it takes time to establish

any kind of business. Please whatever you do, don't
give up. Stick with it and over time you willl see improvement and get better each time you
practice and work you get more experience in what your doing, so

don't worry keep up thw
hard work. Thanks for reading the book. I am Joshua Benjamin Bailey if you would like to contribute like i have, please look up my name online and purchase my book. Thank you for

your time. - Continued: Vlogging is a ver good way to get your message or advertisment across to the viewer. Making your own youtube channel in 2021 is crucial everyone should truly do it. Not only can vlogging be therap utic but they can also help you to increase your daily income.

When you make your own channel on youtube you have unlimted access to the world wide web and everyone on earth who is in it and uses it. Think about it with vlogging you can advertise just about anything you want that is within community guidelines. Making your ow n website to sell your services or goods for consumers is also a very clever idea. Everyone who wants to make extra money online using their com puter really n eeds to have their own website to sell on to profit from, to make more money u sing the internet th an you have ever before. It's important to study your target audience, meanng the people who will be interested in your product or service. Trying new ideas when online i always a good thing to do. Working on a budget is f ine, but I am sure you have also h eared it cost money to make money, well in some case it truly does. So I think it's very important to keep that in mind. Look up Under the table jobs on craigslist.com. Offer your own product or services on craigslist.com. You can also use the app /

website offerup to post services and products on as well. Ebay is a big money maker that you can use to sell things at home you don't want anymore in order to make more money for

yourself. Buying and reselling online can be

some what of a career or at least a good job if you
get good enough at it. Whatever your good at post it online and offer it as a paid service. You
can also, run a service where you downlod a certain number of

music videos from youtube that somebody selects, and send the music videos to them after the payment has gone through. You can dowload mp3's off the intern et of full albums to u se for   pomotional use for you r youtube

music video business. You could download royalte free movies to your computer from the
internet that people request from you
    after seeing your ad online about you tube services. You
can strt online jobs / careers even to   make

more money. A lot of people work through zoom

now a days. Zoom is very important when it comes to business and service online. Zoom can

help you hold business meetings about you r product or service,

zoom can also be used to talk
with possible future clients. Blog's are a good way to talk about subject's online that aren't
talked about very much if at all, but still need to be talked about to help other's with question's

that need answers. By doing this you can earn more respect online, meaning more followers,
meaning more traffic. with more followers and traffic you will have more power to advertise
your product   s. The real way to make a ton

of money online is to start your own bu siness, and come up with your own logo, slogan, merchandise, etc. When you sell your own products and can control the outcome of quantity as well as quality and

you can monoplize on you r product
or be able to keep up with your comp etitors. Sometimes if you look in google search engine for things like free money for example
sometimes you can find websites that are hold ing some kind

of event that is offering free to people who sign up as members to their site for examp le. Going to pawn shop's, yard sale's, garage sale's, moving sales, etc. You might be able to find a item you can buy and resell for prof it on ebay.

Ebay is truly an online money magnet, if you don't h ave an account yet i suggest you get one. Having your own business e-mail that sounds professional is important to people you communicate with so they see you are p rofessional and take your business seriously. You can sell products online that are rare so you can profit fair amounts. So we have learned about the importants of blogging, u sing fou rms, vlogging, creating your own website, writting your own literature to sell on amazon.com or barnesandnoble.com, etc. Just remember some of the most influncel and popular books aren 't even that expensive, go check out prices of popular books online sometime if your thinking about selling literature / books as a product to start your own business with. You can get a good idea at what you think you should price your prou ct at. It's very important to stop over paying for items when you shop online.

Without a VPN the ISP - Internet Service Provider can tell exactly where you are and the ISP also stores all of your data, meaning everything you do the ISP saves it to their database and it

becomes their prop
erty and the company / business can then therfore d o anything they want with you data. Hold on almost their gettting to the point. When the ISP targets everything you
do and records it, the ISP starts to   keep

files on you of how you spend, what you like to eat, what music you listen to, what you like to search in your free tiime, etc. the ISP without a VPN knows everything about you and to save more money online it's important to invest in a VPN so you won't be tracked for what you are searching or doing online. The reason you want to do this is because, when the ISP loses you tracks it can't profile or discriminate against you anymore.

The ISP will have two prices on a identical products for advertisment's online. The ISP will decide on what it knows about you, for example if you have more money the ISP will discriminate and try to charge you more money for a product that is identical sold by one of the companies seperate branches because the ISP keeps tabs and track of it's wifi user's. So if the

company feel's that you spen d more than somebody else that is poorer than you that then you would have to pay more than the poorer person on the company's offer or advertisment of a product or service versus another one of their customers they have one who makes less money so the company th erefore boadcast a cheaper version of the same product or service to the other guy who they know doesn't have as much money or doesn't spend as much money. In my opinion this isn't fair so a tatic to save money and be undetected by the ISP and people who should just mind their own business. When you get the VPN in 2021 it should cost somewhere around $3.50 per month , That's like around $40 a year, to keep from being tracked and targeted, as well as discrimin ated againsst while browsing the web. Getting the VPN will allo w you to ave money in the long run, which equals more cash f rom smart online investin g. Using refference codes or discont's as well help's you to save money online, which inretu rn increases your funds. Capital One Shopping makes saving money effortless. Just add the browser extension and when you check out, they will automatically add the best coupon code in their extensive database to help you save cash. And before you check out at favorite stores like Amazon, Target, Home Depot, and Best Buy, Capital One

Shopping will notify you with a friendly pop-up if the item you're buying is available cheaper somewhere else. Capital One Shopping makes saving money effortless. Just add the browser extension and when you check out, they will automatically add the best coupon code in their extensive database to help you save cash.

And before you check out at favorite stores like Amazon, Target, Home Depot, and Best Buy,

Capital One Shopping will notify you with a

friendly pop-up if the item you're buying is available cheaper somewhere else. Capital One Shopping makes saving money effortless. Just add the browser extension and when you check out, they will automatically add the best coupon code in their extensive database to help you save cash. And before you check out at favorite stores like Amazon, Target, Home Depot, and Best Buy, Capital One Shopping will notify you with a friendly

pop-up if the item you're buying is available cheaper somewhere else. Capital One Shopping is
free to use and will never show you ads. You can add it today if you would like. Capital One

Shopping makes saving money effortless. Just add the browser extension and when you check out, they will automatically add the best coupon code in their extensive database to help you save cash. And before you check out at favorite stores like Amazon, Target, Home Depot, and Best Buy, Capital One Shopping will notify you with a friendly pop-up if the item you're buying is available cheaper somewhere else. Even if you don't have a lot of money to invest, you don't have to let that stop you — you can start investing with $5 or less.

Stash was built to help beginner investors get started. You can buy fractional shares (partial shares) in companies that are household names like Apple, Google, Amazon, and more.6

Normally a single share of these companies could cost hundreds or even thousands of dollars, but you only need as little as $5 to get started with Stash. As a bonus, Stash will give you $5 to invest after you deposit $5 or more into your personal portfolio. Want even more tools and guidance? If you choose the Stash + plan3 when signing up, you can earn 2x stock rewards when you spend on eligible purchases. If you're handy, you take those skills and turn them into cash.

With new projects coming through HomeAdvisor Powered by Angi every two seconds, there's something for everyone. Whether it's painting, mowing lawns, cleaning houses or larger projects like roof and fence installations, HomeAdvisor can connect you to t hese jobs.

HomeAdvisor will set you up with an online business profile and help you collect customer

reviews to land your next job. With over 100 million lifetime service requests and thousands of users searching every day, what are you waiting for? Your opinion matters — but did you know it could also earn you a nice chunk of cash? Branded Surveys lets you get paid for answering simple surveys for Fortune 500 companies like Walmart, Apple, FedEx, and more! But here's the thing: honest opinions are key. These companies depend on your feedback to innovate and produce new products and services. When you complete their surveys, you can get paid a nice chunk of cash . Over 2,000,000 people are doing it, and Brand ed Surveys has paid out over $17,000,000 to date! The best p art? It 's free to sign up and you'll earn 100 bonus points as a new member. Getting started takes less than 30 seconds and you can start earning money as early as today. It sounds crazy. And maybe you're not even sure if it's worth your time. But come on… you're at least a little curious. Getting paid to watch viral videos is a real way to earn cash, and you can do it with a company called Inbox Dollars. No, it's not going to get you rich. Yes... it's probably one of the lowest-effort side hustles. But it's totally worth it if you're just sitting on the couch scrolling anyway. Instead of watching viral videos on YouTube, you could be getting paid actual cash to watch those videos instead. Every little bit of extra money counts. It's simple. You sign up here and confirm your email. Then you watch. Then you earn cash (yes, actual cash… not "points"). And watching these videos whenever you're just chilling on the couch can earn you up to an extra $225 every month. https://www.inboxdollars.com Did you know you can earn money taking online surveys? It's true! You can help brands improve their products and services

AND get paid for your sharing your opinion. Survey Junkie pays you instantly via Paypal to fill out surveys. You can earn up to

$45 per survey. 6 million members and an A+ rating with the BBB can't be wrong – join the crowd and get started earning money! Just searching in google search engine surveys for money can find you a part time job no matter who you are or how old you are.

With making money from survey's not only to you get paid

on time and quickly but it allows you to work at your own pace, or your own hours. Have extra space and want to make money from it? Maybe you've have an unused driveway, garage, basement, shed, or parking spot you want to use for making prof it. If it 's just sitting there, you could turn that unused space into passive income every single month, without ever lifting a finger, Nei ghbor is a web site that lets you rent out your unused space to make extra money on autopilot. Seriously. You just sign up on their site, list what space you happen to have available, and people in your city can rent out your unused space to store their stuff, while paying you a premium for the storage. The entire process works seamlessly and money is deposited into your account automatically. You don't even need to move anything — your renters will move their stuff in (and out) on their own, while you collect a sweet paycheck month after month. Oh, and you're protected by up to $1 million in liability insurance too, sign up today at neighbor.com

Imagine having an extra $5,000 in income this year. What would you do with it? You could pay off bills, slash your debt, and maybe even take a muchLuckily, it ’s not that hard to achieve.While there are plenty of ways to add extra cash to you r bank account, one of the best ways is taking on a side hustle. But with all the junk and scams ou t there, how do you kn ow which opportunities are legit? And how do you know wh ich side hustle can help you earn real money?

FinanceBuzz has you covered. We make it easy for you to get matched with the perfect side hustle that can match your skills, needs, and available time. Stop wasting hours on side hustles out —just answer a few questions and in less than 60 seconds, we'll match you with the perfect side hustle that could help you earn some serious cash on the side.

https://financebuzz.com/best-match-side-hustle?referrer_source

=%2Fways-to-make-extra-money HYPERLINK "https://financebuzz.com/best-match-side-hustle?referrer_source=/ways-to-make-extra-money&offer_id=14218"& HYPERLINK "http s://financebuzz.com/best-match-side-hustle?referrer_source=/ways-to-make-extra-money&offer_id=14218"offer_id=14218

Earning extra cash as a full-service shopper with Instacart is simple - just shop for groceries then

deliver them. Signing up is simple and you can make your own schedule and choose the hours
that work best for you. The best part: You can get paid within an hour of your delivery with their
instant cash out op tion. Instacart can

even tell you which days are the best to work to help you maximize your earnings. Meeting next month's rent is hard.

But canceling that random "it was just a free trial" subscription you signed up for 2 years ago? That's hell, in internet form. And every month that goes by with needless subscriptions means more money draining from your pockets. Here's a secret: sneaky companies like it this way… they purposefully make it hard for you to get rid of those monthly fees. Ugh.

The good news? There's Truebill. Truebill is like your personal financial guardian — in an app. Just con nect you r bank account, and Truebill finds all your recurring subscriptions, cancelling the ones you don't need anymore. They'll even negotiate lower rates on your monthly bills, like phone and internet. Truebill gives you a full view of your financial life in a single screen — from income to spending to saving — so you can start enjoying the hard-earned money you make, and stop wasting it on needless fees.

If you're looking for fast cash to pay off

credit card debt or medical bills or to fund a home improvement project or other major purchase, a personal loan could be a good option. Our partner Personal Loan Pro will match you with loan providers to

fit your specific needs. In only 2 minutes, you could get matched for a loan up to $50,000 and rates as low as 3.49%. Why n
   ot
see if you qualify? Take   advantage of histor   ically low interest rates. It   will NOT affect your credit

score to ch eck rates. Online loans can help you to secure a higher level of finances if you plan to invest wisely and profit from your investment as well as be able to pay back the loan. Even if you're on a tight budget , what â€™s one expense that won't go away? Your grocery bill. Now you can get rewarded for your grocery bills with an app that lets you earn gift cards from pictures of your grocery receipts. All you need is your phone and the

Fetch app. After you're done shopping, just snap a photo of your receipt. Your photo earns points. Then you can redeem those points for gift cards at popular stores like Amazon, Target, and Home Depot. BONUS:

You'll get 2,000 points bonus when you enter this referral code: BUZZ before you scan you r first receipt. We are going a little of topic in the b ook but for it being sold at the lowest p rice possible and is all about money managment and economical improvment mostly using the internet. Have a car, bike, or scooter and want to make some extra cash this month? Look no further than Uber Eats.

With Uber Eats, you can deliver food across town whenever and wherever it works for you and get paid. Just download the app and upload your documents — once you're notified that you 're "active," you can start earning! The best part? You get to be you r own boss. There are no supervisors or minimum time you have to deliver, and you can cash out your earnings up to 5 times a day with Instant Pay. Plu s, you get to keep 100% of your tips, and you could even earn extra with promotion al incentives when delivering during peak hours. With contactless deliveries and the car to yourself, you can roll down the windows, cran k up the jams and start earning whenever you want DoorDash lets you be your own boss and set your own schedule by making deliveries. Customers place an order from the list of restaurants including Starbucks, Chipotle and hundreds of others in your area. The

app then pushes orders to any nearby Dashers who
are logged in. Just pick up the food, drop it off and get paid. You get to keep 100% of the
delivery fee plu s any tips or boosts. Dashers earn an average of $

15- 25 an hour. Due to COVID-19, all orders are no-contact by default. Work as much or as little as you want. You set your hours, so the earning potential is up to you . To b e a Dasher, you'll just need a vehicle, a smartphone, and be over the age of 1 8. These are jobs i am mentioning that you can get online through the internet, that is why i JBB discuss them. I am only extending Dee Power's book as a contributer is so I can upload it as another product to sell on the internet for that good internet money. It had to be a certain length for me to submit the book as a paperback online. The $100 in 24hrs inspired me to finish writing this book to have one more product online, but to also expand on this older model bringing it for th to 2021. I notcied myspace was mentio ned in this book which as well all know unless you live under a rock is outdated. Find you r niche and start earning on the internet everyday. I hope th is book feed's your mind enough to know more about earning money over the inter net sucessfu lly, etc. Woul d $10,000 cash help pay some bills? PrizeGrab is an online sweepstakes website whose mission it is to make sweepstakes simple, easy and fun to enter. PrizeGrab has awarded more than $2,000,000 in prizes to thousands of winners over the last several years! PrizeGrab's huge $10,000 cash sweepstakes ends soon â€" just imagine what you could do with that amount of money. Millions of Americans suffer from diabetes, which can be painful and expensive. But now there is a new way to make a little extra money if you or someone you know suffers from the disease. Cash For Diabetics is a new company that will pay you up to $30 for your unused diabetic test strips. It's as simple as placing your unopened packages in their free mailing kit, and they mail you a check in 2-8 business days. Getting signed up is free and only takes a minute. Stop throwing your unused test strips out and start making some money. It can be tough to get out of credit card debt. With

high APR credit cards, the interest can pile up even if you make a ll your payments on time. With
a little help, you can start making progress and finally see your balances shrink. Tally is an app
that can help you pay off your debt faster.

Just transfer your high-interest credit card balances to a Tally line of credit — a move that could potentially save you hundreds of dollars. Then use the savings to pay down your debt faster. Tally users see an average lifetime savings o f $5,300.8 If you have a credit score of at least 660, it just takes minutes to see howA recent stud y showed that 92% of shoppers b uy online. But what a lot of them don't know is that you can get paid to shop! My Points lets you earn points for each dollar you spend online, which can be turned into gift cards from more than 75 retailers including Amazon, eBay and Walmart. MyPoints members have been awarded over $236 million in gift cards and Paypal cash so far.

They'll even give you a

free $10 Amazon gift card just for making your first purchase. much you could save. Don't worry

- signing up won't hurt you r credit score. Get paid to go shopping with instacart. You can offer services or products on free lance sites like kwork.com and fiverr.com where you can be you own CEO and work your own hours. You can also use these sites to make yourself much more powerful, sense knowledge is power. These sites will allow you to work as well as employe people from across the world of good old earth to work professionally on projects for you for very little money. These sites are online freelancers for hire type gig. They call the job's of Fiverr.com gigs actually. If you have never heard of Kwork.com or

Fiverr.com and your trying to start a succesful business, I suggest you go there, you won't be let down I prom ise. It's a great experience and as far as i know i have never come across a scammer on kwork or fiverr. There are lots of articles out there fu ll of endless ideas on how to make money. But it really doesn't have to be hard, and you don't have to do the typical things like sell your stuff on Craigslist or Etsy, drive for Uber or Lyft, or sort through low-p aying jobs on Fiverr or Mechanical Turk. If you have.If you're spending time on social media, consider switching to one of the ways to make money listed above. You could also commit some of that spare time to taking an online course so you can learn a high-demand freelancing skill. Over time your commitment to making money and improving yourself will pay off an internet connection, you can do just about anything i have mentioned. You can sell your photo's on the internet to people. You can also make short films and sell them onliine. You can also look into starting a Eshop. Always remember how important it is to sell your own product online. You can participate in online research studies. You can provide feedback on social media. You can become a mock online juror. You can earn cash back rewards. You can join online contest. You can also enter a branding contest. You can

---

enter a design contest. You could try a online remote job from your home. Freelance your existing skills for money. You can also learn new skills to use freelancing online. Grow you r freelance business into a agency. You can try being a cam model for https://xhamsterlive.com/signup/ model for example that is a good one. There are other cam model agencies. You can work for yourself, and make you own hours. You can sell your pictures and videos on your site. You can get tips for just sitting and looking into the camera. easy money, very easy and fast . It is a good idea to start a niche website when you can. You can also buy a niche website as well. try to affilate marketing without a web site. you can generate leads for local businesses. You can start a drop shopping business. Resell with amazon FBA. Resell on Ebay, Resell digital products, flip domains, flip websites, Start your own podcast. Build an authority website.

Start a e-mail newsletter. Of course we have tou ched on this but make a ebook and sell it. Create and sell a online course. You could alays try to

make a internet game, or
a mobile game and sell it online. Create or sell music. sell your photo's and video's. You could
start a print on demand business. create and sell you r own private label prod uct.Sell your arts

and crafts online. Mass produce your own physical product to market online. create and sell custom physical products. Crowdfund your physical product. Part of this book literally came from the deepweb / darkweb. It really inspired me to add on to it for the sake of money making online, etc in 2021. License a idea for a physical product. Build marketing software. You can also build a hosting business. Build collaboration software. Build project managment soft ware. Build fremium software. Build niche software. Start a physical products marketplace when you can if your even interested. Build a digital prod uct marketplace. Start a service market p lace. You can also create a free online fourm. Start a paid community. You can also use facebook groups to promote your product's or service. Facebook has a ton of groups that will help you achieve sucess. Day trading / Swinging Trading.

You can also look into forex trading to buy and sell

crypto curren cy. You can look into crypto trading if you want. You can do a Buy & Hold waiting

for a item to increase in valu e, meaning buying and item and holding onto it until it's value goes up for profit purposes. You can look more into robo advisors if your interested. You can work on a dividend income. You can look into real estate investing as well. Look into online video tournaments. You can gamb le or play p oker online in hopes to get more money. But t]taking the survey's is a sure way to make your $100 in around 24 hours of your fully invested time.

Remember the 24 hours doesn't all have

to be in a day it can be broken up or divided into a weeks time, to earn the hundred extra dollars using the internet / wifi. 24 hours split up into 7 days, as around 3 and a half hours per day of nothing but online

work / emp loyment at your
chosen time from you
   r computer, tablet, cellphone, or smart tv. You can also place online bets
with people on all kinds of things, I will let you imagination fill in the blanks. You can try out the

online lottery and try your luck there. You can become a multi-level marketer. Let me wrap t his
up by clearly mapping out the most reliable pat h for you to
 build a successful online business. This comes not only from my own

experience, but also from the experience of 1000's of people I've worked or corresponded with over the years. This is the path of least resistance, the path I've seen work best for most people, so it's likely to work well for you. Step 1 get your income flowing consistently with a Level 2 online business. That means becoming a freelancer or getting a remote job. Those are the quickest and easiest ways to earn a living online, and you can even do a bit of both at the same time. Step 2: As you gain experience, increase your rate and reduce your hours. You want to get to the point where you only have to work 15-20 hours per week, at most, and earn enough in that time to cover all your expenses and have some money left over.

Step 3: Once you get to that point, you're free Now you're earning a comfortable living working

part-time hours, and you can spend all your free time off traveling the world and having loads of
mad adventures (that's what I did initially). Or… you can spend your free time building a Level 3 -

5 business. Because those ARE businesses worth building. Yes, they are more challenging, and yes, they take more time to get off the ground — which is why I don't recommend trying any of

them right out of the gate — but, if you're anything like me, you won't want to play the entrepreneurial video game on easy mode forever. So think of remote work and freelancing as stepping stones — albeit very important stepping stones, but stepping stones nonetheless – to bigger and better online business models. You start small, make things easy on yourself, get some money flowing, free up your time, gain some experience,

and then move on to t
he big
leagues.

www.ingramcontent.com/pod-product-compliance
Lightning Source LLC
Chambersburg PA
CBHW070619220526
45466CB00001B/63